THE OTHER HALF OF HISTORY

THE OTHER HALF OF HISTORY

WOMEN
IN 19TH-
CENTURY
EUROPE

Fiona Macdonald

PETER BEDRICK BOOKS

NEW YORK

Published by
Peter Bedrick Books
156 Fifth Avenue
New York, NY 10010

Text © copyright Fiona Macdonald 1999
Copyright © Belitha Press Limited 1999

Series editor: Claire Edwards
Series designer: Jamie Asher
Picture researcher: Diana Morris
Consultant: Kate Moorse

Printed and bound in China

First American edition 1999

Library of Congress Cataloging-in-Publication Data
Macdonald, Fiona.
    Women in 19th century Europe / Fiona Macdonald. -- 1st
American ed.
      p.   cm. -- (The other half of history)
    Includes bibliographical references and index.
    Summary: Examines the reality of women's lives in
Europe during the 1800s and how change slowly occurred.
    ISBN 0-87226-565-X
    1. Women--Europe--History--19th century--Juvenile
literature. [1. Women--Europe--History--19th century.
2. Europe--Social conditions--1789–1900.] I. Title.
II. Title: Women in nineteenth century Europe. III. Series.
HQ1587.M33   1999
305.4'094'09034--dc21   98-42170
                                                          CIP
                                                          AC

Picture acknowledgments
AKG London: 7b, 12, 14t, 22, 28t, 39, 40.   Bibliothèque
des Arts Decoratifs, Paris/ET Archive: front cover cr.
British Library/Bridgeman Art Library: 33t, 33b.
Simon Carter Gallery/Bridgeman Art Library: 19t.
Cheltenham Art Gallery & Museum, Gloucs/Bridgeman Art
Library: 29t.   Christie's, London/Bridgeman Art Library: 32.
Russell Cotes Art Gallery & Museum, Bournemouth/
Bridgeman Art Library: 37.   ET Archive: front cover cl, 21t.
Mary Evans Picture Library: 6, 8.   Fawcett Library/Mary
Evans Picture Library: 13t.   Getty Images: front cover b, back
cover t & b, 7t, 9b,11t, 11b, 13b, 15t, 16, 19b, 21b, 23t, 25t,
26t, 27, 28c, 29b, 30b, 31, 35t, 35b, 36c, 38t, 41t, 41b, 44t,
44b, 45t.   Haags Gemeentemuseum/Bridgeman Art Library:
19t.   Hartlepool Museum Service/Bridgeman Art
Library: 4b.   Historisches Museum der Stadt, Vienna/
Bridgeman Art Library: 5t.   Josef Mensing Gallery, Hamm-
Rhynern/ Bridgeman Art Library: 38b.   Musée de
l'Assistance Publique, Hôpitaux de Paris/Giraudon/
Bridgeman Art Library: 15b, 24b.   Musée de l'Ile de France,
Sceaux/Giraudon/Bridgeman Art Library: 20.   Musée
d'Orsay, Paris, Peter Willi/Bridgeman Art Library: 24t.
Musée du Petit Palais, Paris/Giraudon/Bridgeman Art
Library: 42.   Musée de St. Denis, Paris/Giraudon/Bridgeman
Art Library: 36r.   Musée de la Ville de Paris/Giraudon/
Bridgeman Art Library: 4t.   Museum Folkwang, Essen/
Bridgeman Art Library: 43b.   Niederoesterr. Landesmuseum,
Vienna/AKG London: 9t.   Private Collection/Bridgeman
Art Library: back cover t, 17t, 34, 43c, 45b.   Private
Collection/ET Archive: 14c.   Retrograph Archive: 5b.
Rochdale Art Gallery, Lancs./Bridgeman Art Library: 23b.
Stapleton Collection/Bridgeman Art Library: 26t.   Tretyakov
Gallery, Moscow/Bridgeman Art Library: 10.   Christopher
Wood Gallery, London/Bridgeman Art Library: 18t, 30t.

CONTENTS

Setting the Scene   4

Learning to Be a Woman   8

Family Life   14

Body and Soul   20

Women as Carers   24

Women at Work   28

Summing Up the Century   40

Fame in a Man's World   42

Glossary and Further Reading   46

Index   48

Changing Europe

People's lives were changing fast in many countries in nineteenth-century Europe. There were new towns, new factories, new political movements, and new ideas. In many parts of Europe, men and women had high hopes of shaping a new world.

> We want to build a new world with you [men], where peace and truth will reign ... we want justice in every spirit and love in every heart.
>
> JEANNE DEROIN, FRENCH SOCIALIST CAMPAIGNER

The Industrial Revolution

From the end of the 1700s and during the 1800s there was a big change in the way goods were produced. There were many new inventions, and new ways of powering machinery. Instead of working on the land or producing goods at home by hand, men, women, and children moved to big new industrial towns to work in factories. These changes began in Britain in about 1775, and quickly spread to Belgium, Germany, northern Italy, and northern France. Factories mass-produced cloth, iron, steel, bricks, pottery, and other goods far more quickly and cheaply than hand workers could. But conditions in the factories were grim. People worked for 12 hours or more at a time, and the work was often dangerous.

Spreading Ideas

Other new technology, such as railways and steamships, made it possible to carry passengers and factory goods further and faster than ever before. Toward the end of the 1800s, inventions such as radios, telephones, and cheap newspapers helped spread news and ideas quickly. Even in southern Europe, where there was little or no new industry, people's lives were changed by new inventions and new ideas.

The city of Hartlepool in northeastern England was a typical industrial city, with a railroad, factories, and rows of workers' houses crowded together. It was also an important port. During the 1800s, overseas trade grew fast. For the first time, many distant peoples came into close contact.

In 1848 there were riots in many European cities. People demanded better rights for workers. This painting shows women guarding a barricade in Vienna, the capital city of Austria.

What About Women?

Most of these changes were brought about by men. Men owned and built factories and organized most political protests. But how did these changes affect women's lives? In this book you can find out about women in nineteenth-century Europe – what they thought, how they worked, and how they spent their days. You can find out how many women campaigned to make life better for themselves and others in those fast-changing times.

This French poster shows women in Africa packing cocoa beans. The beans were shipped to European factories, where they were made into luxury items – chocolate bars and chocolate drinks.

Power to the People

During the 1800s there was growing political unrest in many parts of Europe as people began to question the ways in which their countries were run. Protesters wanted people to have the right to vote. Workers demanded better pay, safer working conditions, and the right to form trade unions. Some people planned new political systems. One of the most famous was Karl Marx, a German who lived in England. He wrote a political pamphlet called the *Communist Manifesto* in 1848. His ideas later inspired revolutions in Russia, China, and other parts of the world.

Europeans Overseas

During the 1800s European governments took control of lands in Africa, India, Asia, and the Caribbean. They claimed the right to take valuable resources such as gold and diamonds from them. European traders also set up businesses there. They imported food, such as coffee and sugar, and raw materials, such as cotton, into Europe to sell at cheap prices. In return, they exported European factory-made goods to these countries.

What Did Women Want?

For many centuries women living in Europe were treated as if they were less intelligent than men. Laws and traditions meant that women did not share the same education, civil rights, and jobs as men. Many intelligent women found this situation hard to bear, as you can see from the protest quoted on the right.

> We have no food for our heads (nothing to think about), no food for our hearts (nothing to inspire us), no food for our activity (nothing to do)...
>
> FLORENCE NIGHTINGALE

Dependent on Men

In 1800 women could not go to college or to most good schools. Without education they could not train to be doctors, dentists, lawyers, or scientists. They could not become priests or church leaders. Women could not serve in the armed forces, and they could not be members of Parliament – most women could not even vote. Married women had no right to own property unless they were widows. In most countries divorce was almost impossible, even if husbands were violent or mad. Because women could not earn much money (their wages were lower than men's), they found it difficult to live independently, and usually had to depend on their fathers or husbands for support.

This cartoon, drawn around 1900, shows the things that men believed filled a woman's mind: marriage, clothes, chocolate, letters, pets, and babies.

Mary Wollstonecraft (1759–1797). Her most famous book, A Vindication of the Rights of Women, *published in 1792, called for women's equality with men. It inspired many campaigners in nineteenth-century Europe.*

"A Woman's Place Is in the Home"

This famous saying describes what most people in 1800 thought was a woman's role. But some women wanted more than this. They wanted to be involved in social and political change. They found ways to make their opinions known, through their relationships with men. Wives discussed politics with their husbands, and mothers gave advice to their sons. A few women went further than this. They wrote books or drew up petitions, protesting against women's unfair treatment, but they were often laughed at, or ignored.

This picture shows the first woman to be awarded a degree in medicine from the University of Berlin, at the end of the nineteenth century.

Slow Progress

Until about 1850 there were few real changes in women's lives. But by the 1860s more women began to leave home to work in schools, offices, and shops, and by 1900 no one could pretend that a woman's place was in the home. Also, by the middle of the century more women began to campaign for women's rights, and especially for education. This meant that women were able to train for new, better-paid careers. Women's protests were not heard or taken seriously for a long time, but gradually they began to win more civil rights. Even so, by 1900, women in most European countries were far from being treated as equals with men. Some people think that they do not have real equality today.

Girls versus Boys

Were women happy to be treated as dolls or flowers, or to spend their lives at home, as the quotes shown right and on page 10 suggest? This chapter looks at how girls were brought up, educated, and expected to behave.

Only a Girl

In theory, parents welcomed all babies into the family. Church leaders taught that children were a gift from God. Many women believed that it was their duty to spend their lives caring for their children, and large families were quite common. This was not always a matter of choice (see page 27), but Queen Victoria in England set the fashion among wealthy families by having nine children.

It's a Boy!

In practice, baby boys were often more welcome than girls. Noble families hoped for a son to inherit the family title and land. Factory owners wanted sons to carry on the family business. Working-class families needed sons who would be able to earn money for the family. Even in the worst-paid jobs, women and girls usually earned less than men and boys. Poor families also found it more costly to care for girls, who were expected to wear neat, clean dresses and petticoats.

> *This little creature is a flower to cultivate, a doll to decorate.*
> ADVICE TO MOTHERS OF DAUGHTERS,
> ALBERTINE NECKER DE SAUSSURE,
> 1838

Artists often painted mothers and babies in a sentimental and idealistic way. Motherhood was seen as the "crowning glory" of a woman's life.

What's in a Name?

Parents chose their baby's names very carefully. Boys might be given a heroic name, such as Victor, which means winner. Often they were also given a family name, which was passed on from father to son over generations. Girls were given sweet, gentle names, such as Mabel (lovable) or Angelina (little angel). Pretty, pure, flower names like Rosa and Lily were also fashionable. In Roman Catholic countries girls were often named after female saints.

Girls were brought up to be quiet, neat, and obedient, but boys had more freedom to go outdoors, get dirty, or make noise. In this family scene from Germany, the boys build a model castle and play with toy soldiers and a gun, while the girls are helping or sewing.

Second-Class Citizen

Girls born in Europe in the 1800s could expect to live very different lives, depending on whether their families were rich or poor. (Compare the clothes and surroundings of the girls shown in the two pictures on this page.) But rich or poor, a baby girl was a second-class citizen from the moment she was born. Young girls had less freedom than boys to study, to travel, to work, to choose how to spend their free time, or to speak openly about their opinions and ideas.

Throughout Europe children from poor families had to go out to work. These girls are working in an English brick factory in about 1830, carrying heavy loads of clay.

9

What the Future Held

In the 1800s boys and girls were brought up in very different ways, to prepare them for different roles when they were grown up. Men were expected to go out to work, but most people expected women to marry and have children. In fact many poor women did go out to work, but this did not affect how people thought women ought to behave. Girls were also taught by their mothers to ignore their own interests and feelings, so they could put other people's needs first.

Feminine Skills

There were a few private schools for rich girls, but they taught skills such as poetry, music, and dancing to help them attract husbands. Girls were not encouraged to tackle subjects such as science and math. In Roman Catholic countries some girls were educated by nuns at convent schools. They learned reading, writing, and skills such as embroidery. Many hours were spent on religious studies, to help the girls become good Christians and dutiful wives.

Love of home, of children, and of domestic duties are the only passions women feel.

Dr. William Acton, 1875

Just for Boys

Until the late 1800s many poor children in Europe, boys and girls, did not go to school full-time. Their parents needed their wages to help the family survive and could not afford to pay school fees. Poor children sometimes went to schools run by charities or churches, held on Sundays or after working hours. Boys from wealthy families went to established schools and to universities. There they learned subjects such as math, science, Latin, and Greek and were prepared for well-paid careers. Girls were not allowed to go to these schools, or to train for professional careers.

Many girls from rich families were educated at home by women teachers called governesses. Being a governess was often a hard and lonely life. But it was one of the few careers for intelligent women who had to support themselves. This Russian painting shows a governess arriving to start a new job.

Girls at a state (public) school in England, 1885. In most state schools throughout Europe, girls learned subjects such as cooking and needlework. In Scandinavia girls studied the same subjects as boys.

State Reforms

In the late 1800s governments in many parts of Europe began to realize that an educated work force would be better for their country. New industries and businesses needed workers who could read and write. So governments began to provide free, or cheap, education for all children in state schools. Lessons were simple: reading, writing, and basic math, with some nature study, history, and geography. Only girls learned cooking, sewing, and housecleaning to prepare them for their future as wives and mothers. Most pupils left school when they were about 12 years old, to start work.

More Changes

By 1900 education was offered to far more children, and most girls went to school. But they were still not given as good an education as boys. For most of the 1800s girls were still only educated to elementary level, and found it hard to go on to study at an advanced level at college or university.

OUTDOOR SPORTS

Many people thought that respectable girls shouldn't do sports. Girls should not run, jump, shout, or become excited. People saw these things as unwomanly.

They were also difficult to do because women wore tight corsets and long skirts. Some doctors said that outdoor activities could injure women's health. (Keen sportswomen pointed out that people didn't worry about women laborers.) In the early 1800s there were few organized sports for women. But after about 1870, when more girls started to go to school, they had the chance to play team games such as hockey. Even so, public sports were still seen as slightly shocking. The first women's tennis championship was not held until 1884, at Wimbledon in England.

The Right to Education

Why was girls' education so limited? Many men believed that women were physically unsuited to study. They thought that too much thinking would weaken them, or even make them go mad. Some people thought that girls were just not smart enough to learn. Many men and women believed that educated women would be unfit for marriage. This idea held a real threat. It was extremely difficult for a woman to survive on her own, so marriage was often essential.

Women Think for Themselves

Luckily, some women refused to listen to these opinions. They set up schools for girls, and campaigned for women's right to go to college. They also helped train hundreds of women teachers who would be able to pass on their knowledge. Women writers helped the education movement by publishing books and newspaper articles about well-educated women and their achievements.

Miss Buss and Miss Beale

In England, two pioneering women, Frances Mary Buss (1827–1897) and Dorothea Beale (1831–1906), decided to give girls an education that was as good as the best education for boys. They set up their own schools and employed women teachers, whom they trained themselves. The girls were taught the same subjects – including math and science – that boys learned.

As Good as the Boys

Helene Lange (1848–1930) was born in Germany. She was trained as a teacher, and at first believed that girls should be taught womanly subjects such as needlework and cooking. But she quickly realized that her girl pupils could learn traditional male subjects, such as math and Latin, just as well as boys. She traveled to England to meet other women pioneers, and returned to Germany to campaign there for a woman's right to the best education.

Helene Lange, pioneer of women's education in Germany. She campaigned to win greater respect for women teachers, and set up private schools to prepare girls for college.

By 1900 Cheltenham Ladies' College, the girls' school run by Miss Beale, had become very successful. This photograph shows Miss Beale, her teachers, and some senior pupils outside the school in 1904.

Feminist and Educator

Barbara Leigh-Smith Bodichon (1827–1891) was a feminist who campaigned on many women's issues, including women's right to own property, to vote, and to have a good education. Barbara's father approved of education for girls and sent her to Bedford College, one of two women's colleges founded in London in the 1840s. Bodichon founded the first feminist magazine in England, called the *Englishwoman's Journal*. Through its pages, she helped many women learn about new feminist movements and ideas. Bodichon married a French doctor, and spent part of each year with him in Algeria and France. Then she came back to England, and devoted at least four months each year to feminist campaigns. She inspired many other women with her energy and bold ideas.

Barbara Bodichon proved by her own achievements that education could help women lead independent lives.

13

Love and Marriage

> My good girl, a grand passion is a grand madness.
>
> CHARLOTTE BRONTE
> A LETTER TO A FRIEND, 1840

Romance was fashionable in Europe in the 1800s. Songs, poems, books, and plays all told stories of true love, or tragic tales of broken promises. Daring new dances, like the waltz, allowed men to clasp their partner's waist. Pretty gifts, such as ribbons, flowers, and newly invented Valentine cards, were popular with girls. Some thoughtful women, like Charlotte Bronte (above), warned their young friends against too much romance, but many parents were happy to let their daughters dream of romance and of living happily ever after.

A pretty Victorian Valentine card.

This romantic picture from Germany shows a courting couple in 1895. But such behavior was frowned on unless a couple was engaged.

A Suitable Husband

For many centuries parents in Europe had made their daughters marry men from families of similar wealth and position. Although by the beginning of the 1800s such arranged marriages were less common, most parents still insisted that their daughters married a man they approved of. They allowed their daughters to daydream about romantic love, but supervised them closely and only allowed them to meet young men from families like their own.

Old Maids

A single woman under 30 could not go anywhere unaccompanied, or be alone in a room with a man who wasn't a relative. Most girls were no longer forced to marry men they disliked, but some parents put pressure on their daughters to marry by telling them stories about the miserable lives led by lonely old maids.

For many women their wedding day was the happiest day of their lives. They hoped for love and companionship, but marriage also gave them a safe place in society. This middle-class couple was photographed in the 1890s.

A Good Provider?

In some ways poor women were less free to marry for love than women from rich families. Although they met many more men, such as male servants, tradesmen, farm or factory workers, and delivery boys, they could not afford to follow their heart. Women's wages were so low that a family needed a man's wage to pay for housing, food, and clothes. Working women hoped to meet a man who was hard-working and had a steady job, then maybe they would grow to love one another after marriage. If a woman did marry purely for love, and not for practical reasons, she risked a life of poverty, homelessness, and hunger.

This French painting shows a single mother leaving the hospital with her new baby. She is stooped and weak-looking. It is snowy, and she is completely alone.

Women Alone

Today many women choose to live alone, to share a house with friends, or set up a home with a partner. These choices would have been impossible for most single women in the 1800s. Except for servants, who received free room and board, and some women from rich families, few women could earn enough money to survive alone. People also believed that it was wrong for men and women to live together without being married.

Poorest of the Poor

Some women did live alone if they could not find a man to marry, if their husbands died or left them, or if they were turned out of their home by their parents. Working women who became pregnant outside marriage lost their jobs, and if they had no help could end up living on the streets. Many of these women were among the poorest of the poor.

Care and Obedience

If you asked any man in the 1800s to describe his ideal wife, he would probably describe her as gentle, loving, delicate, patient, calm, quiet, religious, and totally obedient. She would spend her life caring for her husband and children. She would have no ambitions for herself, and demand no legal rights, but would spend her time at home, creating a peaceful place where he could rest after a busy day at work. She would be what one writer called "the Angel of the Hearth."

A woman's role as the family carer involved everything from managing the household budget to washing her husband when he came home dirty from the factory, coal mine, or fields.

OBEDIENCE TO THE HUSBAND
The woman must obey her husband, live with him in love, respect, and unlimited obedience, and offer him every pleasantness and affection as the ruler of the household.

RUSSIAN LAW CODE, 1836

Laws like this ruled women's lives in many European countries, even if they were not always written down.

Running the Home

Rich women were responsible for running the household. It was their job to hire servants and keep everything in order. Working-class wives usually had to find work to bring in more money. But they were still expected to do all the household chores, and to look after the family. Surveys in the 1890s showed that many working women were tired and run-down. They often went without food and proper clothing, so that their husbands and children would have enough to eat and could keep warm.

Business Partners

In some parts of Europe women worked at home in small, traditional family-run farms, shops, and craft workshops. Husbands and wives worked side by side as business partners, but the husband was always, by law, treated as the head of the firm.

Wives' Rights

Wives in most European countries had few legal rights. But the law gave husbands many rights over them, including the right to beat and imprison them, and to control their children, money, and property. Women could not live apart from their husbands, and were treated unfairly if they wanted a divorce. All through the 1800s women campaigned for reforms in the law, so that they would be treated more fairly.

A 30-Year Campaign

One of the most active campaigners in England was a novelist called Caroline Norton. She had been treated badly by her husband, but when she asked for a divorce, he refused. In 1836 he took her children away from her. He also took all the money she had earned from writing, and the money left to her in her father's will. For the next 30 years Caroline and her supporters fought to win better legal rights for wives. The box (right) shows what they achieved.

This is what many men expected their wives to provide – a cozy, peaceful home where they could relax with their family after a busy day at work.

HOW WIVES' RIGHTS CHANGED IN ENGLAND

1839 Women win right of custody over their children aged under seven, and right of access to older children.
1857 Wives can ask the courts for a divorce from husbands who are cruel, adulterous, or who have deserted them.
1870 and **1882** Wives are allowed to keep their own money and property after they are married.
1878 Wives can demand financial support if they have to leave husbands who have been cruel to them.
1891 Wives can no longer be forced to stay in their husband's house.

Old Age

Most people in the 1800s said that they respected old women. They called them old and wise. They enjoyed poems like the one above, and sentimental paintings. A few old women did command respect. The mothers of rich men held dinners, arranged dances and parties, and wrote letters to their influential male friends. Some families cared lovingly for their older women relatives, but others saw them as an expensive burden. Old, unmarried women were often mocked as useless, childless old maids.

How pleasant it is, at the end of the day [in old age]
No follies to have to repent
But reflect on the past, and be able to say
That my time has been properly spent.

JANE TAYLOR, "THE WAY TO BE HAPPY," 1806

Pictures like this were very popular in Europe. They showed an ideal image of grandparents and loving grandchildren.

This Dutch painting shows the loneliness and poverty of old age. The woman is searching for firewood, because she is too poor to buy coal or logs.

Poor and Powerless

In many ways, old women were the most vulnerable group of people in society. They had few people to help them, and no one campaigned for their rights. Women tended to age faster than men, often because they had given birth to so many children. Women were thought of as old when they were 40. Many women were active long after this, but others became weak, sick, and unable to work. Men were not affected by old age in the same way. Because they often owned property and earned higher wages, it was easier for old men, such as widowers, to marry younger women who would look after them in old age. Poor widows were the least likely group of people to remarry.

Families and Charities

There were no government pensions for old people in the 1800s. Rich women paid for private nursing care, but ordinary women had to rely on their family and friends to help. Some families were kind, others were cruel, and some were too poor to offer help. Parents hoped that their children would care for them in old age, but many children from poor families died young. Unmarried women, and widows with no children, often had to ask for charity or rely on begging to survive.

In the Workhouse

In Catholic countries nuns ran homes to care for the poor. In some countries, such as Britain, the state provided basic care in workhouses. These were designed to help people who became poor through no fault of their own. But workhouses were run like prisons to keep people from using them unless they were desperate. To avoid the workhouse, some older women joined together to rent a shared room, or a corner of a poor person's home. They ran errands, cooked, and did housework to pay their rent. If they got sick, they relied on kindness to survive.

In the 1800s many wives outlived their husbands. If they could afford it, they wore mourning jewelry like this locket. It contains a few strands of hair arranged to look like a feather. The dead person's initials are surrounded by pearls.

In workhouses husbands and wives were separated and sometimes never saw each other again. People were often treated like prisoners.

19

Good Looks, Good Behavior

It affords (gives) to many men quite as keen a delight to see their wives and daughters decked out in absurd costumes ... as it ever afforded (gave) a woman to wear such things.

FLORENCE POMEROY, 1882

Women's fashions changed in the 1800s, but they changed more slowly than they do now. Skirts were always long, but by about 1830 tiny waists and tight sleeves also became popular and stayed in fashion for many years. Rich women wore dresses and hats trimmed with lace, ribbons, beads, fur, and feathers.

Fashion and Finery

Why did women wear such clothes? Partly because they enjoyed keeping up with fashion. Women's magazines, which were still a new idea in the 1820s, showed fashion drawings. Designers in Paris sent dolls dressed in the latest styles to customers all around Europe. But women also wore fine clothes to show off their husband's status. By wearing long silk skirts, tight waists, and jewelry, women showed that they came from a family with lots of money and did not have to do hard physical work.

This French poster, advertising day trips by train, shows a woman and child dressed in the latest fashions at the end of the 1800s. The woman's long hair is pinned in a bun, and the girl has ringlets.

Unnatural Shapes

Mothers taught their daughters that they must suffer to be beautiful. Women achieved a fashionable hourglass-shaped figure by wearing tightly laced corsets, which caused pain and indigestion. In 1857 huge hoop petticoats called crinolines were introduced. They were stiffened with wire or bone, which made it difficult to sit down. Many women died when their skirts caught fire.

Work Clothes

All these fancy clothes were made by skilled women workers. After about 1860, when the first sewing machines were invented, many clothes were made in sweatshops, though the best clothes were still made by hand from luxury materials such as silk and velvet. Ordinary women could only afford simpler clothes, which they sewed themselves from plain, rough fabrics. Even they wore long skirts, tight bodices, and layers of petticoats, though their feet were sensibly clad in thick stockings and heavy boots.

In about 1880 the bustle became fashionable. It was made of heavy padding at the back of the skirt, with the front so tight the wearer could take only tiny steps.

Clothing Reform

In the 1880s a group of women formed the Rational Dress Movement and campaigned against tight corsets and long skirts. They also demanded the right to wear pants. At about the same time, artists designed new, looser gowns – but only a few women wore them. After 1890 bicycling became popular among young women and girls. Cyclists wore loose knickers. Gradually these became acceptable, but only for outdoor wear.

Keeping Clean

For many people, a clean, neat appearance had an extra meaning. They believed they should care for their bodies because they had been created by God. A neat appearance showed a respectful and virtuous character. Girls especially were taught to be pure and clean in thought, word, and deed. Daughters were shielded from anything indecent, such as paintings and sculptures that showed men and women without clothes. Stories and poems that described immoral behavior were banned. Girls were forbidden to swear or to use words such as devil or hell. And no one educated them about human biology or sex.

Long skirts were often impractical for doing many household tasks, but people believed that short skirts were indecent. Even showing an ankle was shocking.

Breaking the Rules

What made a woman "good"? Many men and women in the 1800s would have said deep religious faith, strict morals, purity (ignorance about sex and unpleasant social problems, such as violence against women), neat, modest clothing, and unquestioning obedience to men.

The Woman's to Blame

A few women dared to break society's rules, often because they were desperate. They stole food to feed their children, or ran away from husbands who beat them. Even when women were victims of abuse, they were often blamed. People said they must have been bad wives to deserve such treatment. These women became outcasts, along with divorced women, unmarried mothers, female beggars, and women criminals. Even children, especially girls, born out of marriage were seen as wicked.

Love and Freedom

Some women broke society's rules for different reasons. They wanted to be free. One woman rebel became famous throughout Europe. She was born in France and named Aurore Dupin. She was clever, imaginative, and strong-willed, but her parents arranged for her to marry an older man when she was just 18 years old. She obeyed them, but did not love her husband and was unhappy.

Running Away

In 1831 Aurore ran away to Paris, where she began to write novels to earn money. Her books caused a sensation because her heroines were bold and wild. She described unhappy marriages as slavery, and called for women to have equal rights with men to find love, freedom, and an interesting career. She took a man's name, George Sand, so that people would not ignore her writing as women's work. Sometimes she wore men's clothes because they were more practical and comfortable than corsets and long skirts. Many men hated her because she showed that women could live independently.

George Sand (1804–1876) became friends with some of the greatest writers and musicians of the day.

Womanly Reforms

Elizabeth Fry (1780–1845) challenged society's ideals of good behavior because she wanted reform. She was the wife of a banker and could have lived an easy life, but her religious views made her eager to help others. She began to visit women in prison and was shocked by the conditions she found. Normally, no "good" woman would spend time with prisoners. But Fry organized her friends to provide clean clothes, soap, and water for the prisoners, and to send in food. She organized prison schools and spent hours talking to the women. She believed that, given the chance, most of the women would lead honest lives – a very advanced view for the time. In 1818 Fry advised members of Parliament on new prison designs. She also gave lectures in Europe, to spread her ideas.

JOSEPHINE BUTLER

Butler (1828–1906) was the wife of an English clergyman. Like George Sand and Elizabeth Fry, Butler came from a rich family. Often this kind of background gave women the freedom to rebel against society. Butler wanted to help women who were forced to earn their living by prostitution. Butler discovered that most women who became prostitutes did so because they were desperately poor. Often it was the only way they could earn money to feed themselves or their families. Butler campaigned for better wages and welfare support for all women, and tried to change the laws that punished prostitutes harshly as criminals.

Women and their children in prison, painted in 1878. Elizabeth Fry campaigned for women prisoners to be given clean clothes and bedding, soap and water for washing, and better food. Many women had to bring up their children inside filthy prison cells. Many of them died, from despair or disease.

WOMEN AS CARERS

A Mission

[Women's] mission is the establishment of peace, and love, and unselfishness...
SARAH LEWIS, WOMEN'S MISSION, 1939

Most men and women in Europe were Christians, although there were also communities of Jews and Muslims. Whatever their faith, most people thought it was their duty to worship regularly, say their prayers, read religious books, and do good works. Many women believed that God had given them a special duty, which they called a woman's mission, to bring peace and ease suffering.

In many churches women had to sit apart from the men.

A Minor Role

In most organized parts of the Christian church, women could not become church leaders. Often they were not allowed to sing in church choirs, and had to cover their hair with hats or veils in church. The church also expected women to behave modestly, and support men in their work. But many women were unhappy with such customs. They believed that they had a duty to be more active, and that there was nothing unwomanly about leaving home to help others, even if it meant meeting people who were dirty, diseased, and dishonest.

Nuns often worked in homes or hospitals as nurses.

24

Saving Souls

Many women left Europe to work as missionaries, teaching Christianity to people in Africa and Asia. Others, like Evangeline Booth, wanted to bring the Christian faith to poor people in Europe. Booth was a leading member of the Salvation Army, an organization founded by her father to fight against evil. Salvation Army members worked in slum neighborhoods, providing food, clothes, and shelter for the poorest of the poor.

Sisters of the Poor

In southern Europe, many women became nuns. They provided a network of social services to care for people. They taught in schools, worked as nurses in hospitals, and cared for the elderly and for people with mental illnesses. Many new sisterhoods were set up in the 1800s, including the Sisters of Mercy and the Sisters of the Poor. Their names tell us what they hoped to achieve.

Salvation Army women ran stalls to raise money, selling clothes made in their homes. They also held public meetings to tell people about Christianity and how to fight sin.

Good Works

Women from wealthy families often spent their time doing "good works." They visited poor families and brought them food and clothes. They collected money from friends, held church fairs, and arranged fund-raising dinners and dances. They gave money to set up hospitals, homes for children and old people, and classes to teach working women new skills. Scandinavian women led the way in arranging such voluntary welfare schemes, and women in other countries followed their example. Today people say that these schemes did not prevent the causes of illness and poverty, but many poor families had no other help.

Medicine and Health

Throughout Europe mothers, wives, daughters, and female servants looked after sick people at home, washing and feeding them, and trying to cure them with home remedies, or medicines bought from pharmacies. But even though women were responsible for health at home, they were unable to study medicine or receive any kind of training.

A Bad Reputation

At the beginning of the 1800s most nurses were unskilled and had a bad reputation. But by the end of the century nursing was a recognized profession. This was mainly thanks to a British woman, Florence Nightingale. During fighting in the Crimea, she set out to clean up army hospitals and nurse injured soldiers with more professional care. Back home Nightingale was publicly praised in Parliament. In 1860 the Nightingale School for Nurses was set up, paid for by the public, to give nurses first-rate training in hygiene and discipline.

Elizabeth Garrett Anderson (1836–1917) was the first woman to qualify as a doctor in Europe.

Medical First

Elizabeth Garrett Anderson was the sister of Millicent Garrett Fawcett (see page 41). She was a medical student and a campaigner for women's right to train as doctors. Many women did not like being examined by male doctors, and so did not seek medical help. Anderson particularly wanted to care for women. English law did not allow women to go to medical school, but Anderson discovered a legal loophole that allowed her to train as a pharmacist and do some medical work. British doctors changed the rules to stop her. She finally qualified as a doctor after leaving Britain to study in France.

Sophia Jex-Blake (1840–1912) faced threats from the other students when she tried to study medicine at college.

Sophia Jex-Blake

When Sophia Jex-Blake attended medical lectures at Edinburgh University in 1869, students and lecturers objected that it was not "proper" for women to study bodies in the same room as men. Students brought sheep into the room, saying that all lesser animals could enter the room now that women were there. Jex-Blake fought for her right to study medicine for the next four years. Then the university had a law passed by Parliament making her efforts illegal. Finally she went to study in Switzerland, where she gained her degree, and a license to practice as a doctor in Ireland.

A Long Struggle

Male doctors did not want women to join their profession. They banned women from studying medicine at college, and from qualifying as doctors. After a long struggle, women in many European countries did win the right to become doctors, and to train students of their own. But by 1900 there were still only about 1,000 women doctors working in Europe.

Trained nurses in about 1890. They are wearing their nurse's badges, which show that they are qualified, on a ribbon around the neck.

MEDICAL GAINS

1865 In England Elizabeth Garrett qualifies as a pharmacist, the only medical qualification open to women.
1865 The universities of Berne and Zurich, Switzerland, allow women to train as doctors.
1868 The University of Paris allows women to study medicine.
1872 Women are allowed to train as doctors in all Russian medical schools.
1874 Elizabeth Garrett (now Garrett Anderson) and Sophia Jex-Blake set up the London School of Medicine for Women.
1876 The British government passes a law allowing women to train as doctors.
1882 Spanish student Pilar Taurengi and three other women complete their medical studies at college, but are not allowed to qualify as doctors.
1899 The first women in Germany complete their medical studies. They are not allowed to practice until 1900.

Birth and Death

Pregnancy and childbirth were the most dangerous times in a woman's life. Throughout the 1800s childbirth was the main cause of death among women. Wives were often frightened when they found they were pregnant, but could do little to avoid having babies because they there was no cheap, reliable form of contraception. Many people thought that birth control was wrong, but pioneers such as Aletta Jacobs, in Holland, and Annie Besant, in England, were determined to help other women. Besant faced prosecution when she tried to publish a leaflet giving advice to ordinary women in 1877. Jacobs opened the world's first birth control clinic in Holland in 1882.

WOMEN AT WORK

Working in the Home

Throughout the 1800s housework was done by women. They worked either as servants in wealthy family's houses, or looked after their own homes. Except for a few specially trained male servants, men did not cook, clean, or care for children. In most countries, men who helped around the house were despised.

A German housewife giving orders to her cook. Besides planning menus, women kept accounts of the money they spent on food.

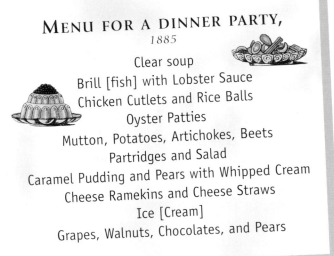

MENU FOR A DINNER PARTY,
1885
Clear soup
Brill [fish] with Lobster Sauce
Chicken Cutlets and Rice Balls
Oyster Patties
Mutton, Potatoes, Artichokes, Beets
Partridges and Salad
Caramel Pudding and Pears with Whipped Cream
Cheese Ramekins and Cheese Straws
Ice [Cream]
Grapes, Walnuts, Chocolates, and Pears

Fresh Food

In the 1800s there were no freezers or refrigerators, so food had to be bought fresh from local shops, or brought from farms and gardens almost every day. Many foods were only available at certain times of year. Planning meals, cooking, and storage were much more difficult than they are today. You can see a rich family's menu above.

Not Just for Fun

In 1861 English cooking writer Mrs. Beeton wrote that managing a household was like commanding an army. A rich woman spent many hours organizing servants and arranging dinner parties for important guests. For her female friends she arranged lunches, tea parties, kaffee-klatches (coffee-and-cake parties) and at-homes (afternoon parties with tea, coffee, fruit, candy, and ice cream, and sometimes live music). All this entertaining was not just for fun. By making sure her guests had a pleasant time, a good hostess helped her husband make useful business contacts, and her children make suitable friends.

This is a well-equipped kitchen from the 1890s. Food was cooked on the iron kitchen range, which needed cleaning and filling with coal every day.

Clean and Decent

Wherever they lived, most women worked hard to keep themselves and their families clean. Wealthy women employed servants to clean their homes and wash and iron their clothes. Ordinary women had to perform these tasks themselves. Poor women sometimes took in washing from other families, or had cleaning jobs to earn a little cash.

Many families did not have kitchens. Housewives, like these French women, washed clothes in a nearby stream or pond.

Washday Chores

Without hot running water, or electric machines, washing was a hard job. Water for washing was brought from wells, backyard taps, or pumps in the street, then heated on coal-fired ranges or in huge copper vats over an open fire. Clothes were washed by hand in tubs using scrubbing brushes and soap. They were wrung out by hand, or squeezed between wooden rollers in a hand-turned mangle. In warm, sunny weather, they were spread outside to dry, but in the winter they often took several days to dry indoors. Finally, clothes were ironed with heavy metal flatirons, heated over the fire.

This sentimental painting shows a girl leaving her home and family to take a first job as a servant. Servants often began work when they were only 13 or 14 years old.

LIFE AS A SERVANT

The maid of all work should get up at six ... she will light the furnace and the fires or get the stove going. She will brush the clothes and clean the shoes. She will clean the bedrooms, put water in the water closets, carry up wood and coal, empty the lavatories, and carry the waste downstairs. She will tidy the dining room and wash the breakfast dishes and put them away. Before preparing lunch, she can do a special chore for each day of the week, for example, on Saturday, thoroughly clean the kitchen, on Monday, clean the living and dining rooms, on Tuesday, clean all the brass and copperware, on Wednesday, do the washing, on Thursday, the ironing...

FROM A BOOK OF INSTRUCTIONS FOR FRENCH SERVANTS, 1896

Life as a Servant

There were about twice as many women servants in Europe as men servants. Most families could afford only one or two servants – a maid and a woman cook. Male butlers, footmen, coachmen, and gardeners were employed only in big houses. Life as a woman servant was hard. Although they were given room and board, their wages were very low. They had no guaranteed holidays. Employers often allowed servants to visit their families for a week once a year, but they did not have to. Servants might go on vacation with their employers, but they had to work in the vacation home, too.

The Working Day

The working day started before dawn, and often did not finish till midnight. Servants had to obey orders without questioning, be silent unless spoken to, and never sit down in the presence of their employer. They were not allowed to leave the house without permission. If they were late getting home on their one half-day a week off, they might be locked out. They were not allowed to meet boyfriends at the back door, and if they did they risked dismissal.

Finding Friends

A servant's life could be lonely. Life was often better for women working in big houses where there were more servants. They could make friends and share worries, though sometimes young girls were bullied by older staff members. They also had the chance to learn new skills, such as cooking and fine needlework, which might help them find a better job in another house. Some families treated their servants kindly, but most took them for granted, and a few were cruel.

Sweeping and Polishing

Caring for any house was hard work. Floors and stairs had to be swept, scrubbed, and polished. Rugs had to be carried outside and beaten; paintwork and windows had to be cleaned. Sheets, towels, and curtains had to be washed and mended by hand. Harsh soaps and scouring powders made women's hands rough and sore, with chapped, bleeding skin that could take weeks to heal. Long hours spent scrubbing floors caused an injury called housemaid's knee. Many servants damaged their backs carrying water or coal up flights of stairs. Kitchen sinks, bathtubs, and chamber pots all had to be cleaned with soap, water, and scrubbing brushes.

Lightening the Load

Toward the end of the century, factories began to make easy-to-clean ceramic bathtubs and sinks. Chemists invented new household cleaning products. In wealthy homes, people had elegant new bathrooms, with water heaters and toilets that flushed. Kitchens had clean, piped water, and stoves that heated water. Inventors designed gadgets to make housework easier, but only a few rich families could afford these.

Young servants photographed at the end of the century. Working as a servant in a family house or hotel was one of the only jobs for uneducated women.

Working in the Country

Country women worked hard alongside men, whether at home, in rural industries, or in the fields. Even though new farm machines, such as reapers and threshers, were invented during the 1800s, many farming tasks were still done by hand. In northern Europe there were brickyards and coal mines where women and girls did dangerous jobs, sometimes underground.

Producing Food

Food played an important role in the lives of many country women, but it was not a pleasant one. They worked long hours in the fields. In the winter their clothes were drenched with rain and snow, their boots and skirts were caked with mud, and they were chilled to the bone by winds. In the summer, they were hot, tired, and sunburned, and their eyes and noses were clogged with dust. Even the hardest digging and carrying often had to be done by hand.

Migrants and Gangs

Women often found jobs as farm laborers, moving from place to place picking grapes, hops, apples, or potatoes. Women laborers might be organized and paid for by male gang-masters, who hired them out to farmers. Gang-masters whipped women and girls who were too tired or sick to work. Women were often harassed by male farm workers, and there were no toilets, or separate places for the women to sleep.

This French painting shows potato pickers. Digging sunbaked soil by hand and bending to pick up potatoes all day was dirty, tiring work.

Women in a small workshop in about 1800. They are spinning and winding woolen thread. By the end of the century, tasks like these were carried out by steam-powered machines in towns.

Many Jobs

During their lives, country women might have several different jobs. Before they married they might work in a mine, or as part of a gang. After they married, they had to care for their families, but also needed to work to bring in money. Sometimes they became the breadwinner if their husbands got sick or were injured at work. They found work to do at home, such as lacemaking, embroidery, braiding straw to make hats, cleaning feathers for quilts, and collecting twigs to make brooms.

Cottage Industry

Working at home was often tiring and poorly paid. Well-meaning upper-class women often encouraged cottage industries, especially needlework, to give poor women the chance to earn money. The women were glad to have the work – it was better than starving – but sitting still and sewing for long hours in dark, drafty cottages often led to bad backache and ruined eyesight.

Managers and Wives

Country women married to wealthy men led comfortable lives, but they still had many responsibilities. The wives of rich landlords, and owners of large farms and vineyards, worked hard managing servants in the house and on the farm. On smaller farms, the farmer's wife was often in charge of her own farm-based businesses, such as keeping bees for honey, and making butter and cheese.

Selling farm-produced food was usually women's work. This Dutch picture shows a well-to-do farmer and his wife. She is selling butter from a big wooden barrel.

Working in Towns and Cities

Between 1800 and 1900, millions of men and women in northern Europe left the countryside to work in industrial cities and towns. Country wages were low, farm work was seasonal, and living conditions were often bad. People moved to the cities, hoping to find regular work in newly built factories, in ironworks and coal mines. With more money they hoped to be able to afford better housing.

Factory Work

Most women found work in factories making goods such as fabric and clothing, boots and shoes, or pottery. In all these trades, most of the workers were women, though most of the supervisors were men. Employers liked women workers because their small, nimble fingers were better suited than men's to many tasks. They were more obedient than men, too, partly because of the way they were brought up, and partly because they were frightened of losing their jobs. Many children relied on their mother's earnings to survive.

Women workers in a British factory, 1834. They are tending steam-powered looms (machines that weave cloth). The woman at the front of the picture is about to reach into her machine, perhaps to join some broken threads. Many serious accidents happened this way.

These French coal miners are wearing wooden clogs, and hoods and aprons made of burlap to protect them from coal dust. In many countries, women worked alongside men in dirty, dangerous jobs.

Boring and Unhealthy

Factory work was tiring, boring, and unhealthy. In the early 1800s the working day started at 5:00 A.M. and might not end until 7:00 P.M. Factories were hot, dirty, smelly, and noisy. Women and children lost fingers or were crushed in fast-moving machines. In cotton mills, dust caused lung disease. In ironworks and pottery factories, chemicals such as white lead poisoned many women and their unborn children.

This dramatic picture shows a woman factory worker, poisoned by white lead. It was produced as part of a newspaper campaign to improve health and safety for women workers.

A Better Way of Life?

In 1893 Clementina Black, a woman trade unionist, said that if she were the mother of girls, she would rather they worked in a factory than as servants. This seems to be a strange comment. But Mrs. Black said that although factory work could be harder, and very rough, factory girls could live at home, close to their families and friends. They had more freedom than servants to do what they wanted, even if their parents were strict. They might, for a while, have a little money to spare for new clothes, candy, or occasional days out with their friends. They would never be so free or well-off again. Once they left home and got married, their lives would change.

Lower Wages

Although factory work gave young women some spending power, on the whole their wages were much lower than men's. Employers and male workers argued that because men were heads of households, only they needed to earn a family wage.

In 1888 women workers in a London match factory went on strike to protest against dangerous machinery and miserably low wages. Feminists protested that these women were treated like slaves.

LOUISE MICHEL

Louise Michel (1830–1905) was born in France. She was trained as a teacher, but found it almost impossible to live on a woman teacher's pay. She joined the socialist movement, which was inspired by the communist writings of Karl Marx. In 1871 she took part in a workers' revolution called the Paris Commune. She was arrested, locked in a cage, and exiled to an island in the Pacific Ocean.

United for Action

Throughout the 1800s men formed trade unions to campaign for better working conditions and more pay. Women were not usually allowed to join. Men were afraid that women would bring the wages down. So women began to form trade unions of their own. This happened first in Britain, because factory working developed there first. In the 1780s and 1790s groups of British working women set up "friendly societies" to give some welfare help to the members. From the 1830s onward there were local unions for women in different factories, and even some strikes. But the unions were weak and could not rely on men's unions for help. Emma Paterson set up the first national women's trade union in Europe in 1874, to give a network of support for all women workers.

Changes in Europe

All over Europe women also became involved in newly formed political parties, especially those with socialist or communist views. Often (like Louise Michel, above) they chose this way to protest, rather than joining a trade union. But by the 1880s there were active women's unions in most European countries. By the early 1900s more than a million women had joined a union.

THE SONG OF THE SHIRT
With fingers weary and worn
With eyelids heavy and red
A woman sat in unwomanly rags
plying her needle and thread.
Stitch! Stitch! Stitch!
In poverty, hunger and dirt;
And still, with a voice of dolorous pitch
She sang the Song of the Shirt...
Work – Work – Work
My labour never flags;
And what are its wages? A bed of straw,
A crust of bread and rags.

A POEM BY THOMAS HOOD, 1843

The Song of the Shirt

Coal miners and factory workers were not the only people to suffer bad working conditions. Thousands of skilled needlewomen worked long hours at home, or in cold, damp workshops, sewing fine clothes for big clothing companies. Often they were given so little time to complete their work that they had to sit up all night, and were paid so little that they could not afford enough food, or fuel to heat their rooms. Working in dim candlelight ruined their eyesight. In 1843 a popular English magazine launched a campaign to help home workers. It published pictures of half-starved needlewomen, and a poem called *The Song of the Shirt*.

Health and Safety

Thousands of women workers were injured every year. In England, from about 1842, and in Germany from about 1869, laws banned women from working alongside men in some of the most dangerous jobs, such as mining. By 1913 most countries had similar laws. But some women did not want these laws. They said women should have the right, like men, to work where they chose, and that there should be better conditions for both men and women.

This picture of an exhausted needlewoman was painted in 1887. It shows her working in a dark, cold attic. The painting is called Weary, *or* The Song of the Shirt, *after the poem (above).*

New Jobs for Women

Before 1800 many women in towns took jobs based on their traditional role of providing food and home comforts for men. They worked as waitresses, barmaids, and cleaners in bars and hotels. They took in washing and ironing, and rented rooms to lodgers. Even though the work was exhausting, most people thought of it as unimportant and unskilled, so the women who did these jobs were badly paid. These jobs continued, but after about 1860 there were also new jobs for women in offices and shops.

This Dutch painting shows a waitress in a bar, in about 1870. She is on her feet, carrying and serving all day. As part of her job she has to look cheerful, even if she is tired or ill.

Madame Boucicault made her store very comfortable to attract rich customers with plenty of money to spend on clothes, food, and luxury items.

Shops and Stalls

For centuries women had run, or helped run, shops – often in the front room of their family home. They also sold things from market stalls, or from baskets by the side of the road. These ways of selling continued, but as industrial towns grew bigger, more shops were opened to sell items being mass-produced in factories. Most of these shops were owned and managed by men. But the world's first department store, called Au Bon Marché, in Paris, was planned and managed by a businesswoman named Marguerite Boucicault. Her husband provided the money, but she had the idea of selling lots of different things in one store, and making it luxurious, so people would be tempted by the displays. The store was opened in 1865.

We open at 5:30 and close at 12:30 (after midnight). We have to inhale smoke, gas (from lamps), and the foul air from the numbers crowded at our bar, and we have no comfort, release, or relaxation from the dreary wearing toil. I assure you we all feel fit to drop with fatigue...
BARMAID, 1876

38

Ladylike Work

As more stores opened, many more young women began to work as salesclerks. People often believed that working in a store was more ladylike than working in a factory. But clerks in large stores spent 12 hours a day (or more) on their feet, and were not allowed to sit down. Store owners were supposed to provide clerks with food, but often this was only bread and tea.

Office Jobs

Toward the end of the century there were many new jobs for educated women from ordinary families. Most of these were in offices, where women worked as secretaries, printers' assistants, and mail clerks. After typewriters were invented in about 1880, many women became skilled typists. Compared with work as a cleaner or a servant, office jobs were fairly well paid. Women earned enough to live away from home and have some freedom. Women were hardly ever given jobs as managers, and if they married they had to leave their jobs.

REASONS FOR EMPLOYING WOMEN AS TELEGRAPH CLERKS
suggested in 1871 by
Frank Ives Scudamore, when he reorganized the British post office.

- Women have quick eyes and ears.
- Women are more patient at being shut in a confined space.
- Well-educated women will work for lower wages than well-educated men.
- Women are often very good at spelling and writing neatly.
- Women are less likely than men to join together to protest about low wages.
- Women are likely to get married. They can then be forced to leave their jobs. So the Post Office will not have to provide them with a pension.

Telegraph clerks (above) sent and received messages using special telegraph machines and arranged for their speedy delivery.

A German lawyer and his secretary, photographed in about 1890. She is wearing typical clothing for a professional woman – a long dark skirt with a white blouse and tie.

SUMMING UP THE CENTURY

In 1792 campaigner Mary Wollstonecraft (see page 7) begged men, on behalf of women everywhere, to "snap our chains" and be happy with women's friendship rather than slavish obedience. Had Wollstonecraft's hopes of freedom been realized by the year 1900?

Equality with Men

In all European countries men still earned higher wages, owned more property, and had better education and more personal freedom. They also had more political and legal power. By 1900 women in Europe still did not have the right to vote. But, thanks to women's efforts during the century, progress toward equality had been made. The biggest changes were in women's work and education. By 1900 many more women had paid work outside their homes in factories, shops, offices, and hospitals. Almost all women were given some education, and a few went to college. A few women had professional careers, for example as lawyers, doctors, and teachers.

Why So Slow?

Change came slowly, partly because many men could see no reason to give up their power. They felt that there was a natural or God-given order to the way society was organized. There was also no united women's movement with clear aims. Instead, women all across Europe protested about many different problems and tried to win freedom in different ways.

> The real question is, whether it is right and expedient [useful] that one half of the human race should pass through life in a state of forced subordination to the other half.
>
> HARRIET TAYLOR MILL, 1851

Clara Zetkin (left, 1857–1933) campaigned for women's rights in Germany. Rosa Luxemburg (1871–1919) came from Poland. She moved to Germany and campaigned for women's rights, and also called for a workers' revolution.

40

MILLICENT GARRETT FAWCETT

Millicent Fawcett (1847–1929) was an early campaigner in England for women's right to vote. She helped set up many local societies to campaign for women's rights, and became president of the National Union of Women's Suffrage Societies in 1897. Although she often faced angry words and harrassment, Fawcett was determined to campaign only by peaceful means. Women in Great Britain did not win the right to vote on the same terms as men until 1928, the year before Fawcett died.

Different Means to an End

In Russia, Germany, and France the most active campaigners for women's rights were also political campaigners. These women believed that political, even violent, revolution would set women free. In Germany, Clara Zetkin was a communist and a campaigner for women's rights. She was trained as a schoolteacher and founded a political newspaper for women. In Britain and Scandinavia, campaigns for equality were led by women who preferred a slower approach, and disliked violent protests. Swedish writer Fredrika Bremer (1801–1865) used novels to campaign for women's rights, children's welfare, and international peace. In Roman Catholic countries such as Italy and Spain many women were guided by their priests, who taught that campaigning for equality was wrong.

Working Together

The earliest campaigners, such as Mary Wollstonecraft, acted as individuals. They put forward ideas rather than action plans. As women began to set up trade unions, hold meetings, and run letter-writing campaigns, they gained practical experience of politics and organizing protests. By working together, they gave their demands strength. After 1860 the right to vote in national elections on equal terms with men became one of the most important issues for campaigners, especially in northern Europe. More and more women joined the suffrage movement. Finland was the first European country to give women equal voting rights, in 1906.

Emmeline Pankhurst (1858–1928), third from the left, took the fight for women's suffrage in Britain into the 1900s. In 1903 she founded the militant Women's Social and Political Union. Her followers were called suffragettes. They held protest meetings, smashed windows, and went on hunger strikes.

41

FAME IN A MAN'S WORLD

Women Outside the Home

Before 1800 it was almost impossible for women to have an independent career. They did not have the same chance as men to study or develop their skills. Rich women learned to dance, sing, play the piano, and paint, but they were not expected to make careers of these activities. During the 1800s there were more chances for women to follow a professional career. Even so, they needed good luck and determination to make their way. On the next four pages you can read about some of the women who were successful and won fame in a man's world.

Sarah Bernhardt

SCIENCE, TRAVEL, AND ADVENTURE

Science was a man's subject in the nineteenth century. Education campaigners made some changes over the century, but by 1900 there were still very few women scientists. Only a few women had the money to pay for long years of study, or had husbands who were willing to support them. Women were also not expected to be adventurous. If they traveled at all it was with their families, to enjoy the culture and good air around Europe. Young women were definitely not expected to travel alone to explore distant parts of the world.

MUSIC, ART, AND WRITING

Many people thought that actresses, singers, and dancers belonged to a glamorous but immoral world. But going on the stage was one of the few careers that was open to all women, no matter what their background was. Actresses lived a rootless life, traveling from theater to theater, and appeared on stage in heavy makeup and daring costumes. But a talented performer really could rise from rags to riches, and win fame and praise.

SARAH BERNHARDT (1845–1923)

The French actress Sarah Bernhardt (below left) was known by her admirers as the "divine Sarah." She starred in many plays written especially to display her passionate style of acting. She even performed a man's part, when she played Hamlet in Shakespeare's play of the same name. Bernhardt also painted, wrote poetry, and managed several theaters. She performed in Europe, the USA, South America, Egypt, and Australia, and won praise wherever she went.

MARIE TAGLIONI (1804–1884)

Italian ballerina Marie Taglioni was born into a family of musicians and dancers. This helped get her career off to a good start, but her success was due to her own special skills. She created a whole new way of dancing. Delicately balanced on the tips of her toes, she looked as light as air. She was pale, dark, long-legged, and extremely thin, and her looks and way of dancing had a huge influence on ballet style.

CLARA WIECK (1819–1896)

It was easy for women to feel that they had to sacrifice their careers for their family. German musician Clara Wieck had to make this difficult decision. She was a talented composer and pianist. But when she married another composer, Robert Schumann, she gave up writing her own music and giving concerts because she believed she should support her husband's work and stay at home with him. Clara only began to perform in public again when her husband became ill and died, leaving her with children to support.

JENNY LIND (1820–1887)

Swedish singer Jenny Lind was just one of many women singers who became famous across the world. She toured widely in Europe and America and became known as the Swedish nightingale, because of her high, pure voice. Unlike many performers, she did not have a rich, luxurious lifestyle. Instead, she gave much of the money she earned to charity. When she retired, she settled in England and became a singing teacher.

From left to right, Anne, Charlotte, and Emily with their brother, Branwell.

THE BRONTE SISTERS

Charlotte Bronte (1816–1855) and her sisters Emily (1818–1848) and Anne (1820–1849) were daughters of a clergyman. They grew up in wild countryside in northern England. All three worked as badly paid teachers in small, private schools. They had plans to open a school of their own, but this never happened because they did not have enough money. Charlotte, Emily, and Anne all wrote poems and novels. They read them aloud at home and encouraged each other to send them to a London publisher. They signed their work with men's names, so they had more chance of being published. They called themselves Currer, Ellis, and Acton Bell. After her first books were published, Charlotte visited London. She met and became friends with many famous writers of the time. Her most famous novel is *Jane Eyre*, which is still popular today.

Mary Shelley (1797–1851)

Mary Shelley was the daughter of Mary Wollstonecraft (see pages 7 and 41). Shelley was a writer and historian, and knew many important poets and thinkers of her day. Her private life caused a scandal when she ran away to live with a poet called Percy Bysshe Shelley. Today she is remembered for writing the book *Frankenstein*, about out-of-control science.

George Eliot (1819–1880)

Like other women writers, English author Mary Anne Evans chose a male name. She came from a wealthy family and was intelligent and strong-minded. She shocked society by living with a man who was separated from his wife, and began to write novels to support him and his children. In her writing she highlighted how people could be trapped by society's rules.

Rosa Bonheur (1822–1899)

Bonheur was a painter's daughter and studied with some of the best art teachers in France. She specialized in painting animals. To make sure her paintings were accurate, she studied animals, alive and dead. The Paris police allowed her to wear men's clothes to visit slaughterhouses, so she could study the animals more closely.

Berthe Morisot (1841–1895)

Morisot was a French painter and one of the pioneers of Impressionism. Like other girls from wealthy families, she was given drawing lessons. But she broke society's rules by becoming a professional artist. Even though she was happily married and had a daughter, she continued with her career and became famous, especially for her paintings of women in everyday settings.

Julia Margaret Cameron (1815–1879)

Cameron was a British pioneer photographer. She experimented with new scientific techniques to create sensitive close-up portraits. She used soft focus and dramatic lighting to create her pictures, especially of women, children, and famous people.

Marie Sklodowska Curie (1867–1934)

Marie Curie (below) was born in Poland. At first she worked as a governess, sending money to her sister, who was studying in France to be a doctor. When her sister had finished her studies and was married, she sent for Marie to join her, and paid for her to go to college. Marie was a brilliant student. In 1895 she married French scientist Pierre Curie, and they worked together. In 1898 they discovered two chemicals, which they called radium and polonium. They won the Nobel Prize in 1903 for their work on radioactivity. When Pierre was killed in a traffic accident, Marie continued their work. She was given Pierre's job (the first woman to work at the Sorbonne University in Paris) and became a professor in 1908. She worked until her death in 1934.

MARY SOMERVILLE 1780–1872

Somerville (above) was a Scottish mathematician, geographer, and astronomer. As a child she was taught art, needlework, and dancing, but longed to read books on mathematics and geography like her brothers. A clergyman brought her copies of two math textbooks, and she studied them secretly at night – until the servants complained that she was burning too many candles, and her mother stopped her from reading in bed. When Somerville married, her husband also disapproved of her "wasting time" on math. But after he died in 1807 she began to study again. In 1817 Somerville remarried. Her second husband was proud of her and encouraged her studying. By 1834 her work was so widely admired that she was given a yearly sum of money by the government. She also joined other women to campaign for the right to vote. Somerville continued to write important scientific work for the rest of her life.

ISABELLA BIRD BISHOP (1831–1904)

British explorer Isabella Bird Bishop (below) spent her early years bored and ill. She was advised by doctors to travel abroad to rest. Instead she set off on a series of adventures, visiting Australia, New Zealand, and the Sandwich Islands (present-day Hawaii). In the USA, she climbed the Rocky Mountains, slithering across ice sheets in long skirts. When she returned to England, Isabella married and began to write books and articles about her travels. Her husband died after only five years, so she set off again and became the first European woman to visit parts of Malaysia and Japan. She made her last long journey at the age of 69, traveling on horseback through the heat and dust of Morocco. In 1892 she became the first woman to be made a fellow of the Royal Geographical Society.

GLOSSARY

article (newspaper) A short piece of writing, giving news or views.

barricade A barrier across a street, put up by protesters.

birth control Precautions people take against becoming pregnant.

bodice The upper part of a woman's dress.

campaign An organized group of activities, such as speeches or marches, designed to change people's views or win new rights. (To campaign is to take part in a campaign.)

career A job with opportunities for progress, training, more responsibility, and more pay.

citizen A person who is a member of a community and has political rights within it.

civil rights The rights that allow ordinary people to play a full part in society, such as the right to vote, receive an education, have a job, marry, and follow their own religious faith.

class divisions A way of grouping people by their social status, their jobs, and how rich they are. **Working-class** usually refers to manual workers.

communist Someone who believes in a system of government where there is no private property and no class divisions. Instead, the government owns and runs everything on behalf of the people.

corset A piece of clothing that made a woman's waist look slimmer by binding it tightly.

culture A society's customs, beliefs, and artistic traditions.

custody The right to take care of someone.

dismissal Being sent away, or losing your job.

export Goods sent out of one country and sold in another.

feminist Someone who wants women to have equal rights and equal opportunities with men.

governess A woman who works as a teacher in a family home.

imports Goods brought into one country from another. (To import is to bring goods into the country.)

Impressionism A style of painting that created images using patterns of color, light, and shade, instead of hard lines. The Impressionists were a group of painters in France in the late 1800s.

influential Having power to change opinions or make things happen.

legal rights Rights that can be demanded by law.

mass-produced Made in large quantities in factories.

militant Aggressive and outspoken, especially when supporting a cause.

missionary A person who tries to convert others to his or her own religious beliefs.

movement (political) A group of people working together to gain social or political change.

old maid In the nineteenth century, the name for an unmarried woman more than 30 years old.

petition A document containing a list of demands. (To petition is to ask for changes to be made or needs to be met.)

pioneer Someone who explores or settles new land, or who develops new ideas or inventions.

private school A school where parents pay for their children's education.

protests Demands for change. A protester is someone who demands change.

qualified Having the right education, training, and skills for a job.

reforms Changes that bring improvements.

revolutionary Wanting to make big changes in society and government, by force if necessary.

socialist Someone who believes in a system of government where ordinary people have a say in how their country is run, and wealth is shared equally by everyone.

state school A school run by a government, where people don't have to pay for their education.

status Someone's position in society – how they are seen in relation to other people, as more or less important.

suffrage The right to vote in political elections. A suffragist is someone who believes in extending suffrage to more people. In the second half of the nineteenth century, the term was usually applied to women who wanted the vote.

suffragettes The women who fought for the vote from the beginning of the twentieth century.

survey A collection of information or opinions.

sweatshop A crowded, unhealthy workroom.

technology New scientific developments and ideas that are used to modernize an area such as industry in a practical way.

trade union A group of workers who have joined together to demand better pay and working conditions.

welfare scheme An organized plan to improve someone's living conditions, providing better healthcare and everyday support.

women's issues Subjects such as healthcare or legal rights that affect women as a group.

FURTHER READING

Ashby, Ruth, and Deborah Gore Ohrn, ed. *Herstory: Women Who Changed the World* (Viking, 1995)

Bridenthal, Renate, Claudia Koontz, and Susan Stuard, ed. *Becoming Visible: Women in European History* (Houghton Mifflin, 2nd edition, 1987)

Heller, Nancy. *Women Artists: An Illustrated History* (Abbeville Press, 1987)

Kalman, Bobbie. *19th-Century Girls and Women* (Crabtree Publishing, 1997)

Levy, Patricia. *Women in Society: Britain* (Marshall Cavendish, 1993)

Lerner, Gerda. *The Creation of Feminine Consciousness: From the Middle Ages to 1870* (Oxford University Press, 1993)

Miles, Rosalind. *Women's History of the World* (Harper Collins, 1990)

Rose, Phyllis, ed. *The Norton Book of Women's Lives* (Norton, 1993)

Steffof, Rebecca. *Women of the World: Women Travelers and Explorers* (Oxford University Press, 1992)

Trager, James. *The Women's Chronology* (Henry Holt, 1994)

INDEX

actresses 42, 43
Anderson, Elizabeth Garrett 26
artists 42, 44

Beale, Dorothea 12, 13
Bernhardt, Sarah 42, 43
Besant, Annie 27
birth control 27, 46
Bishop, Isabella 45
Black, Clementina 35
Bodichon, Barbara 13
Bonheur, Rosa 44
Booth, Evangeline 25
Boucicault, Marguerite 38
Bremer, Fredrika 41
Bronte sisters 43
Buss, Frances Mary 12
Butler, Josephine 23

Cameron, Julia Margaret 44
careers 40, 42, 46
carers, women as 16, 24-27
charities 19
childbirth 27
childhood 8-13
Christianity 24-25
city work 34-39
cleanliness 21, 29
clothes 20-21, 29
colleges and universities 6, 10, 12, 13, 27
communist ideas 5, 36, 46
cottage industries 33
country work 32-33
Curie, Marie 44

doctors 26-27
Dupin, Aurore 22

education 6, 7, 8-13, 40
Eliot, George 44
entertaining 28
equality 7, 40, 41
Eugenie, Empress of France 45

factories 4, 34-36
family life 14-19
farm work 32-33
fashions 20-21
Fawcett, Millicent Garrett 41
food 28, 32
Fry, Elizabeth 23

governesses 10, 13, 46

health 26-27, 35, 37
housework 16, 28-31
husbands' rights 17

Industrial Revolution 4

Jacobs, Aletta 27
Jex-Blake, Sophia 27

Lange, Helene 12
Lind, Jenny 43
love 14-15, 22
Luise, Queen of Prussia 45
Luxemburg, Rosa 40

marriage 6, 12, 14-17
medicine 26-27
Michel, Louise 36

missionaries 25, 46
Morisot, Berthe 44
musicians 42, 43

names, choosing babies' 9
needlewomen 37
Nightingale, Florence 26
Norton, Caroline 17
nuns 24, 25
nursing 26-27

obedience 16
office work 39
old age 18-19
old maids 14, 18, 47
overseas trade 5

Pankhurst, Emmeline 41
Paterson, Emma 36
political change 5, 36
poor people 8, 9, 10, 15, 18, 19, 25
prison reforms 23

rich people 9, 10, 18, 19, 25, 33
romance 14
royal women 45
rules, breaking society's 22-23

safely 37
Salvation Army 25
Sand, George 22
schools 6, 10-13
scientists 42, 44, 45
servants 30-31
Shelley, Mary 44
shop work 38-39

single women 14, 15
socialist ideas 36, 47
Somerville, Mary 45
Song of the Shirt 37
sports 11
suffragettes 41, 47

Taglioni, Marie 43
technology 4, 47
town work 34-39
trade unions 5, 36, 47
traveling abroad 42, 45

Victoria, Queen 45
voting rights 41

wages 36
washing 29
welfare schemes 25, 47
Wieck, Clara 43
wives' rights 17
Wollstonecraft, Mary 7
work 7, 9, 16, 28-39, 40
work clothes 21
workhouses 19
writers 42, 43, 44

Zetkin, Clara 40, 41